Destined for
GREAT Things!

WORKBOOK
A guide to self-improvement,
self-reflection & self-development

Dr. Mia Y. Merritt

Copyright © 2009 by Mia Y. Merritt, Ed.D
All rights reserved. No part of this book may be reproduced in any form, except for the inclusion of brief in a review, without permission in writing from the author or publisher.

Library of Congress Control #2009907179
ISBN: 978-0-9720398-1-9

Destined for Great Things Workbook

Library of Congress Cataloging-in-Publication Data
Merritt, Mia

Printed in the U.S.A. by
Morris Publishing
3212 East Hwy 30
Kearney, NE 68847
1-800-650-7888

Dr. Mia Y. Merritt

Dr. Mia Y. Merritt was born and raised in Miami, Florida where she attended elementary, middle, and high school. She matriculated and graduated from Florida Memorial University with a Bachelor's Degree and Nova Southeastern University with Master's and Doctorate Degrees. She is an Author, Assistant Principal, College Professor, and Inspirational Speaker. She has always had a love for acquiring knowledge and sharing knowledge. As a result of her good and bad encounters with life, she wrote, edited, and published her first book, *Destined for Great Things* in 2007. Her second book, *Prosperity is my Birthright* was released in 2009. The workbook that you are holding, *Destined for Great Things Workbook* is a guide to self improvement, self-reflection & self-development. It is very thought-provoking, but will help you to identify and bring forth all the great things there are inside you.

About this Workbook

Hello my friend,

Before you continue turning the pages of this workbook, you must be willing to "be" the following things:

- Be equipped to do some writing
- Be mentally prepared to do some thinking
- Be emotionally stable to do some deep soul searching
- Be true to your inner self
- Be psychologically ready to face your hidden fears
- Confront the things that have hindered you from moving forward
- Identify your gifts, talents, skills and abilities

This workbook is an interactive, hands-on, thought-provoking guide about YOU! It is designed to bring up and out the greatness that has been placed inside you, but may not have been watered, cultivated or nurtured because of neglect, fear, apathy, or abandonment. This workbook will help you to meet the person you really are, show you how your thoughts and words have magnetized certain people and situations to you and motivate you into taking charge of your life through goal-setting and planning. As you take this journey, you must be mentally prepared to meet yourself face-to-face while delving into this workbook. Good luck!

If you complete all the activities in this interactive workbook, I promise that you will have a closer, enlightening, more meaningful relationship with the new person that you will have met, YOU!

Are you ready? Set? Let's go.

Table of Contents

About This Workbook IV

Chapter 1: Develop Good Habits 1

Chapter 2: A Spirit of Excellence 7

Chapter 3: Find the Good in Every Situation 13

Chapter 4: Laugh Often 21

Chapter 5: Control Your Emotions in Every Situation 29

Chapter 6: Live Today as Your Last Day on Earth 37

Chapter 7: Believe That You Are a Miracle 45

Chapter 8: Plan for Prosperity and Abundance 54

Chapter 9: Examine Each Night Your Deeds of the Day 63

Chapter 10: Pray With an Attitude of Gratitude 69

> There is a light within you that shines from God.
> As you encounter the trials and difficulties of life,
> the darkness disappears because of this light,
> but you must walk boldly with
> confidence, assurance, and motivation.
>
> *Dr. Mia Y. Merritt*

Week 1

Develop Good Habits and Practice Them Daily

*As a child I was slave to my impulses, now I am slave
to my habits. My actions are ruled by emotions,
love, fear, hate, appetite, environment, and habit.
The worse of these elements is habit.
Therefore, if I must practice habits, let me practice
good habits. My bad habits must be destroyed and new
fertilizer laid for good seed.*

*Both success and failure are the result of habit.
Successful people practice the habits that
failures do not like to practice.
Good habits will never produce bad results.
Bad habits will never produce good results.
Only a habit can overcome another habit.
In the beginning, I make my habits,
but in the end, my habits make me.*

*I will get into the habit of rising early,
praying daily, talking less,
listening more, smiling often,
and speaking positive in all manner of conversation.*

*As I develop good habits and practice them daily,
they become a pleasure to perform.
If they are a pleasure to perform, it is my nature to
perform them often.
When I perform them often, they become a habit,
and I become their slave,
and since they are good habits, then this is very good.*

> *Excellence is not a singular act, but a habit. You are what you repeatedly do.*
>
> Shaquille O'Neal

Developing Good Habits

BACKGROUND:
A bad habit is any act performed so often that it becomes automatic. If you consider a frequent action to be unpleasant then it is labeled a "bad habit" (i.e. lateness, oversleeping, thinking or speaking negatively, smoking, using profanity, wasting time, etc.). The first step in breaking a bad habit is to look at why you find this behavior so compelling. In other words, what is the payoff for doing this seemingly negative thing? Habits are never eliminated. They are replaced by a new, hopefully better habit. In order to overcome a bad habit, you must create a new one to replace it.

A. If your desire is to eliminate a bad habit by replacing it with a good one, then think of a good habit now and prepare action plans needed to make that new habit automatic.

B. If you have no bad habits, but your desire is to add a good habit, then think of the new habit now and develop the action plans needed to start this new habit, making it automatic.

Part A: (If you have no bad habits, then skip part A and go to part B)

1. List two of your bad habit(s) on the lines below:

   Habit 1 _____

   Habit 2 _____

2. How often do you perform this/these habit(s)?

   Habit 1 _____

   Habit 2 _____

3. How do you feel as you are performing this/these habit(s)?

   Habit 1 _____

   Habit 2 _____

4. What makes you perform this/these habit(s)?

   Habit 1 _____

   Habit 2 _____

5. Why have you not eliminated this/these habits up to this point?

   Habit 1 _____

   Habit 2 _____

6. What do you think it will take for you to stop doing this/these habit(s)?

   Habit 1 _____

   Habit 2 _____

Part B:

1. If your desire is to replace a bad habit with a new one, then list the new habit(s) that you will develop in place of the bad one(s). If you have no bad habits, but would like to develop a new good habit only, list the new habit(s) on the lines below:

   Habit 1 _____

   Habit 2 _____

2. How often do you plan on performing your new habit(s)? Be specific. (i.e. every morning, afternoon, evening, each time I have the urge to perform the old habit, etc.)

   Habit 1 _____

   Habit 2 _____

3. When will you start your new habit(s)?

   Habit 1 _____

   Habit 2 _____

5. How will you motivate yourself to do it every day?

Habit 1 _____

Habit 2 _____

It has been said that anything done for 30 consecutive days becomes a habit. Therefore, you must strive to perform your new habit for at least 30 consecutive days. Don't think about or focus on the bad habit at all. Keep your motivation on the new habit. If you miss a day, don't get discouraged, just pick up where you left off and resume from there.

6. I will start on this day: _____

Each day that you perform the new "good" habit, put a checkmark (√) in the box for that day. Each day that you do not perform the "bad" habit, you will shade in the box until you have shaded the old habit away. Remember, stay committed. Good luck!

MAKE THE APPLICATION

DAYS	OLD HABIT	NEW HABIT	DAYS	OLD HABIT	NEW HABIT	DAYS	OLD HABIT	NEW HABIT
1.			11.			21.		
2.			12.			22.		
3.			13.			23.		
4.			14.			24.		
5.			15.			25.		
6.			16.			26.		
7.			17.			27.		
8.			18.			28.		
9.			19.			29.		
10.			20.			30.		

Successful people are successful because they form the habits of doing those things that failures don't like to do.

Albert Gray

My Lessons Learned on "Developing Good Habits"

Motivation is what gets you started. Habit is what keeps you going.

Jim Rohn

> God seeks expression through us each and every day and He expresses Himself through men, women, and children.
>
> *Dr. Mia Y. Merritt*

Week 2

A Spirit of Excellence

*The person who is constantly hesitating between
which of two things he or she will do, will do
neither. If you waver from plan to plan, goal to goal, and
constantly bend back and forth in the wind like a lily, you will
never accomplish anything great or useful.
It is those who concentrate on but one thing at a time
who advance in this
world.*

*Not many things scattered, but one thing whole heartedly is the
demand of our world. If you scatter your efforts, you will
not succeed. Decide on your goals and keep them forever
in your thoughts until they have been ultimately achieved.*

*One of the great joys of life comes from doing everything
you attempt to do to the best of your ability. There is
a special sense of satisfaction; a pride in reviewing such a work,
a work, which is accurate, full, exact, and complete in all its
parts, which a mediocre person who leaves his or her work
in a half-finished condition, can never know.*

*The smallest task well done becomes a miracle of achievement.
Accomplishment of whatever kind is the crown of effort,
the result of thought. You cannot pursue a worthy goal
steadily and persistently, with all the powers of your mind,
and fail. Work in a spirit of excellence in all you do..*

ACTIVITY #2

> *Mediocrity anywhere is a threat to excellence everywhere.*
>
> *unknown*

A Spirit of Excellence

BACKGROUND:

When each small task is performed in an efficient, well-organized and competent manner, it becomes a miracle of achievement. Small tasks become bigger tasks and when bigger tasks are performed in a spirit of excellence, you become known as a person of worth who knows how to get the job done! The great difference between those who succeed and those who fail does not consist in the "amount" of work done by each, but the "quality" of the work. Whatever you start to do, you must finish. Whenever you start something and do not finish it, you are forming the habit of failure. Whenever you start something and complete it with excellence, you are operating in a spirit of excellence.

    A. Do you strive for excellence when you do things, or do you operate in mediocrity by doing only enough to get by?

    B. Is there talent in you that you are holding back from coming forth in your life?

Part A:

If you do only enough to get by, list some things that you can change by enhancing the quality of your actions in those areas (i.e. waking up earlier, creating a "to do" list, staying later at work, following up on tasks, spending time with children, etc).

1. _____
2. _____
3. _____
4. _____
5. _____

How often are you willing to work in a spirit of excellence on the things that you listed above? Be specific. (i.e. daily, three times a day, once, twice, three times per week, every chance I can, etc.)

I will start on this day: _____

> *KEEP IN MIND:*
> *Anything done for 30 consecutive days becomes automatic. Therefore, you must perform your new habit for at least 30 consecutive days. If you miss a day, don't get discouraged; just pick up where you have left off.*

Each day that you work in a spirit of excellence, surpassing the minimum, put a checkmark (√) in the box for that day.

Make the Application

1. _____   11. _____   21. _____
2. _____   12. _____   22. _____
3. _____   13. _____   23. _____
4. _____   14. _____   24. _____
5. _____   15. _____   25. _____
6. _____   16. _____   26. _____
7. _____   17. _____   27. _____
8. _____   18. _____   28. _____
9. _____   19. _____   29. _____
10. _____   20. _____   30. _____

Part B:

1. What gift, talent, or skill do you have which you are not allowing to express in your life?

    a. _____

    b. _____

    c. _____

2. Why do you think you have not allowed this talent or skill to express through you up to this point?

   a. _____

   b. _____

   c. _____

3. What can you begin to do **today** to start expressing your talent or skill?

   a. _____

   b. _____

   c. _____

4. What do you think will be the benefit of expressing this talent or skill on a consistent basis?

   a. _____

   b. _____

   c. _____

5. What do you think will be the result of **not** expressing your talent?

   a. _____

   b. _____

   c. _____

6. What is your fear of expressing your skill or talents?

_____

_____

_____

_____

My Lessons Learned on
"The Spirit of Excellence"

We must overcome the notion that we must be regular. It robs you of the chance to be extraordinary and leads you to the mediocre.

Uta Hagen

Successful people tap into their creative powers through being alone in the silence, which is where all the power is. Managed solitude pays off. When the mind is peaceful and still, it catches a glimpse of the greater good.

Dr. Mia Y. Merritt

Week 3

Find the Good in Every Situation

Look at all things with love and become renewed.
Speak with love. Behave with love. React to the actions
of others with love.
Face each day and every person you meet with love,
and love yourself.

Love the sun because it warms you.
Love the rain because it cleanses your spirit.
Love the light because it shows you the way.
Love the darkness because it shows you the stars.
Welcome happiness because it enlarges your heart.
Endure sadness because it opens your soul.
Acknowledge rewards because they are your due.
Welcome obstacles because they are your challenge.

Find the good in every situation!

How should you speak?
Extol your enemies and they will become friends.
Encourage your friends and they will become brothers and sisters.
Always dig for reasons to applaud.
Never look for excuses to gossip.
When you are tempted to criticize, bite your tongue.
When you are moved to praise, shout on the roof!

Find the good in every situation!

> **If you don't like something, change it. If you can't change it, change the way you think about it.**
> *Mary Engelbreit*

Find the Good in Every Situation

BACKGROUND:
When we learn how to look past appearances to perceive truth, our perspective about things and people change. We often look at the natural appearances of things and form our opinions from there. As human beings, our wisdom and knowledge is limited and as limited beings, we tend to think error. We think things to be true that really are not. We must look for the good in everything, and in searching for the good, we are searching for the truth and we will find it.

   A. Do you have a tendency of solidifying your opinion of people or situations after hearing only one side of a story?

   B. After experiencing difficult situations, do you seek for the lesson learned from the experience?

Part A:

1. On the lines below, recall a situation where you formed a judgment about a person or situation and later found your opinion to be inaccurate or your judgment to be passed in error.

_____

_____

_____

_____

_____

_____

2. How did you feel after finding out the truth of the matter?

_____

_____

_____

3. What will you do in the future to prevent the natural tendency to form quick judgments after hearing only one side of a story?

_____

_____

_____

4. How will you try to perceive truth in all situations, which goes far beyond appearances?

_____

_____

_____

5. On a scale of 1-10, how inclined are you to believe the details of a situation told to you by a friend or family member?

1 2 3 4 5 6 7 8 9 10

> **Be Mindful of This:** *Consider the source and remember: The other person involved in the story you hear has family members and/or friends who believe the details of their story, which may be contrary to the story you heard. Where is the truth? How do we perceive truth?*

Meditation is a valuable skill when exercised effectively. Meditation is the process of going into the silence to clear one's mind in order to concentrate upon a particular ideal. Going into the silence through meditating is to go where the power and answers are. The most powerful forces in the universe are silent. Electricity, heat, love, ingenuity, creatively, intuition, and motivation are all silent, yet they are all powerful, dynamic, and dominant. We may meditate to acquire power and perceive truth as well. When we learn how to concentrate on the self within and allow the truth to be brought to us, it will come.

Wisdom is perceiving truth.

Make the Application

Find a place in your home where it is quiet and free from distraction. Take a comfortable position where you can sit erect, without leaning or slouching. Be perfectly still and close your eyes. Focus only on the silence for five minutes. As you blend with the silence, repeat in your mind the following words: <u>God is truth. I am truth. God and I are truth.</u> Say this 20 times in your head as your eyes are closed. Repeat this exercise everyday for 2-3 days. This helps focus your mind on one thing. For the days remaining, focus on clearing your mind of any and all thoughts. Let power, intuition, and insight come to you. Expect them to come and receive them when they speak to your mind and spirit. Start with five minutes. Gradually increase the time by five minutes every five days. At the end of the 30 days, you should be at 30 minutes. You will find that as you search for truth, it comes to you and your day-to-day activities take on a brand new perception.

5. On the lines below, write the amount of minutes that you spent in meditation. You will begin to feel results if you do this every day. Your time should increase by five minutes every five days:

1. _____	11. _____	21. _____
2. _____	12. _____	22. _____
3. _____	13. _____	23. _____
4. _____	14. _____	24. _____
5. _____	15. _____	25. _____
6. _____	16. _____	26. _____
7. _____	17. _____	27. _____
8. _____	18. _____	28. _____
9. _____	19. _____	29. _____
10. _____	20. _____	30. _____

Part B:

After encountering difficult situations, do you seek for the lesson learned from the experiences?

One the lines below, find "*good*" that can come out of the scenarios below:

1. A father/husband loses his job with no other income to support his family.

_____

_____

_____

2. A daughter has to take a leave of absence from work to care for her mother who has Alzheimer's Disease.

_____

_____

_____

3. A car breaks down on the way to an important appointment.

_____

_____

_____

4. A doctor tells a patient that she has breast cancer.

_____

_____

_____

5. A family of sons, daughters, grandchildren, nephews and nieces sit at the bedside of a grandmother in her final moments before she passes away.

_____

_____

_____

6. A young girl is heartbroken over the boy she loved breaking up with her.

_____

_____

_____

On a scale of 1-10 how easy was it for you to recognize something good that could come from the situations above?

1 2 3 4 5 6 7 8 9 10

Perception is Reality to the one Perceiving.

Look at the picture for about ten seconds. What do you see, a young lady or an old lady?

At first glance most people see a young, seemingly elegant "young" lady, but if you were to look a little closer for several more seconds, you would see a very old-looking woman with a seemingly sad countenance. Most people call this an optical illusion, but an illusion is a delusion or false impression or appearance. This picture is no illusion. There is really a young woman in the picture and there is also an old woman depicted in this picture. It all depends on what you choose to see.

It is the same with you and how you perceive things. Some people see a glass as half empty, while others see the glass as half full. Always remember that perception is reality to the one perceiving. Try to always see the better side of things, because that will then become your reality.

My Lessons Learned on
"Finding the Good in Every Situation"

Plant the seed of meditation and reap the fruit of peace of mind.
Remez Sasson

As busy as we all are, we are each given the same amount of hours in a day. What we choose to do in those hours determines what we shall have to do in the next 24 hours to come, just as the use we have made in past time has fixed our place in present time.

Dr. Mia Y. Merritt

Week 4

Laugh Often

*No living creature can laugh except human beings.
Only we have this gift of laughter, and it is ours to use
whenever we choose.*

*When you smile, your digestion improves. When you chuckle,
your burdens are lightened. When you laugh, your life is lengthened,
for this is the great secret to long life, and now it is yours.*

Can you laugh when confronted with person or deed who offends you
so as to bring forth your tears or makes you want to curse? Certainly!
Four words you can train yourself to say until they become a
habit so strong that immediately they appear in your mind whenever
good humor threatens to depart from you.
These words will carry you through every adversity and maintain
your life in balance. These four words are:
THIS TOO SHALL PASS.

*For all worldly things shall indeed pass.
When you are heavy with heartache, you shall console yourself with,
"This too shall pass."
When you are puffed up with success, you shall warn yourself with,
"This too shall pass."
When you are burdened with wealth, you must tell yourself,
"This too shall pass."
If all worldly things shall indeed pass,
why should you be of concern for today?*

> A smile starts on the lips. A grin spreads to the eyes. A chuckle comes from the belly; but a good laugh bursts forth from the soul, overflows, and bubbles all around.
>
> *Carolyn Birmingham*

Laugh Often

BACKGROUND:

"*A day without laughter is a day wasted,*" said the comedian Charlie Chaplin. Every few months, stories seem to emerge about laughter and its benefits to health. Doctors are just beginning to understand what happens in the brain when we laugh. Laughter is the result of something funny or humorous. Constant laughter comes from a happy person. A happy person is the result of a contented person with a positive outlook on life, things, and people. A positive outlook is the result of understanding the creative power of positive thinking.

A. How can we function in a consistent state of positive thinking?

B. What things can we put into place to begin training the mind to think positive about ourselves and the world around us?

Part A:

An affirmation is an ideal that is developed of the person you aspire to be. An affirmation repeated frequently forms the conception in your mind of who you shall become in the very near future. As you visualize yourself being this person, you eventually will become what you visualize. Focusing on your ideal self helps you to think positively, and this strategic thinking begins to crystallize into your physical world.

An affirmation speaks of the roles you play in the lives of those around you, the virtues you posses, the services you render, the habits you perform, the actions you take, and the thoughts you think.

Take a look at the author's affirmation on the next page. On the lines that follow, begin to write your own affirmation.

Mia's Personal Affirmation

I Mia Yvette Merritt, am a prosperous, spiritual, humble, and faithful woman of God with character and integrity. As a child of the most high and powerful God, I meditate on the Word day and night. I pray without ceasing and I worship God in spirit and in truth. I exhibit a quiet and meek spirit, which in the sight of God is of a great price. I walk in this world with humility and grace, and yet I am confident and fearless. Out of my mouth departs wisdom, power, and the law of kindness. I control my emotions in every situation, I practice good habits on a daily basis, I attract and magnetize to me the people, circumstances, money, and conditions that I require in order to fulfill and achieve my highest ideals. I am great! I come from greatness!

I attract greatness, and I am the kind of person

I want to attract into my life.

God has blessed me with great wealth which I give back to Him in the form of tithes, offerings, service, and financial blessings to others. As a faithful steward, I spend wisely. I seek guidance from God continuously before making life-changing decisions, and I patiently wait for His answer to be placed into my spirit. I have over $50,000 saved for emergencies and rainy days. I am a lender, not a borrower. I am above and not beneath. I am the head and not the tail.

It is my birthright to live in prosperity, peace, harmony, and abundance and my life is a reflection of that birthright. I speak with perfect self-expression and my words rapidly perform those things which I speak.

I keep my mind, my spirit, and my soul healthy by reading books that feed me in an effort to increase in knowledge, wisdom, and understanding. Knowledge is pleasant unto my soul, therefore discretion and understanding preserves and keeps me. I attain unto wise counsel concerning the plans that I have set for my path. All of my positive thoughts are being established. My daily mindset is one of constructive thinking, ingenuity, and absorbing the power and wisdom of the mind Christ.

As a mother, sister, and friend, I encourage, uplift, and speak life into the situations of others, and bless them with the fruit of my lips. I am highly favored and respected of others, and I am of a trustworthy spirit. I speak what the spirit of God gives me to speak, and I do it in season, and in love. My children arise and call me blessed; and my husband also, and he praises me. Favor is deceitful, and beauty is vain, but a woman who loves the Lord, she shall be praised!

Make the Application:

Write your own personal affirmation.
Use as many sheets of paper as needed to write it.
This is the ideal person that you want to become.

Personal Life Affirmation for:

_____

> *After you have written your affirmation, make several copies of it. Post one up in your bathroom so that you can see it in the mornings. Take one with you to work so that you may read it at your leisure. Keep one in your notebook, so that as you think about it, you can ponder upon it. Continue to repeat this affirmation everyday until it becomes a habit so strong that your subconsciousness picks it up easily. You will soon see how you start becoming this person. You will begin to attract people, circumstances, things, and events to you resulting from the powerful words that you are putting out into the universe.*

Part B:

What things can you put into place to begin training your mind to think positive about yourself and the world around you? What are some things you can do to bring laughter and joy into your life?

1. On the lines below, write three things that you can do or places you can go to have a good time and bring laughter and joy into your life.

   a. _____

   b. _____

   c. _____

2. Who are the people that you would share this pleasurable time with?

   a. _____   d. _____
   b. _____   e. _____
   c. _____   f. _____

3. Why did you choose those (above) people to share your laugher and joy with?

   _____
   _____
   _____

4. What is stopping you from doing this in the very near future?

   _____
   _____
   _____

On a scale of 1-10, how likely are you in the very near future to do the some of, if not all the things you listed?   1 2 3 4 5 6 7 8 9 10

PLEASE ANSWER THE FOLLOWING QUESTIONS USING THE RUBRIC BELOW:

5 –Always   **4**– Almost Always   **3** –Sometimes   **2** –Almost Never   **1**–Never

1. I take time to write down the goals that I want to achieve. _____

2. I review my goals at least once per week. _____

3. I do something towards accomplishing my goals at least every week. _____

4. I take the time to meditate. _____

5. I spend time in prayer at least once weekly. _____

6. I feed my spirit by studying and reading the bible at least once weekly. _____

7. I attend worship service at least twice monthly. _____

8. I take the time to read books to feed my mind and spirit. _____

9. I take a least one vacation per year. _____

10. I hang out with friends at least monthly. _____

11. I spend "quality" time with my family at least once each month. _____

12. My family and I eat dinner at the dinner table together weekly. _____

13. I am content and satisfied on my current job. _____

14. I desire to change from my current position. _____

15. I make sure that I get adequate physical exercise at least twice weekly. _____

16. I make sure that I eat properly and manage my diet daily. _____

17. My bills are paid on time each month. _____

18. I am able to save money without touching it at least monthly. _____

19. I examine my thoughts daily to ensure that they are positive. _____

20. The mental attitude that I exhibit daily is pleasant. _____

ADD UP YOUR SCORES AND REFER TO THE ANSWERS BELOW.   SCORE=

81-100 (High) Congratulations! You are living your life to the fullest with balance, enjoyment, stability, and apparent joy! (May I hang with you?)

61-80 (Pretty High) Well done! You are making and taking time to live life with fulfillment and balance although there is a little room to add more.

41-60 (Average) It is good that you manage to keep your life maintained, but there is much room for improvement. Expand your consciousness.

21-40 (Low) Life is meant to be lived and you are not living it. You must begin to start living your life with purpose, meaning, and satisfaction.

Below 21 Now this is just sad. ☹

As you review your answers, look at the areas in which you have the lowest scores and decide how you plan on improving those areas. The rubric was created by asking questions in the following areas.

1. The first three questions dealt with **goal setting**.
   The next four had to do with your **spiritual** life.
   The next sentence dealt with feeding your **mind**.
   The next four related to **family and recreation**.
   The next one had to do with your **current job/career**.
   The next two was **health**.
   The next two was in the **financial** area.
   The next two was your **mental attitude**.

2. My lowest scores (1s and 2s) were in: (Put a checkmark)

   ____ Goal setting
   ____ The spiritual area
   ____ Family/recreation
   ____ Job/career
   ____ Health
   ____ Financial
   ____ Mental Attitude

   I plan on doing the following to increase my actions in this/those areas: _____

3. Please write your goal and action plan for the areas that you scored a 1 or 2 in.

Area Needing Improvement: _____

Goal: _____

Action plan _____

To be completed or increased by (Date)_____

Area Needing Improvement: _____

Goal: _____

Action plan _____

To be completed or increased by (Date)_____

Lessons Learned on "Laugh Often"

The person who knows how to laugh at himself will never cease to be amused.

Shirley MacLaine

Week 5

Control Your Emotions in Every Situation

All nature is a circle of moods and I am a part of nature and so like the tides, my moods will rise, my moods will fall.

I will remember that every adversity carries with it the seed of tomorrow's victory and every sadness carries with it the seed of tomorrow's joy. I will master my emotions so that each day will be positive, for unless my mood is right, my day will be a failure. I will do this by learning the secret of the ages: "Weak are they who allow their thoughts to control her actions; Strong are they who force their actions to control their thoughts."

Each day when I awaken, I will follow this plan of battle before I let the forces of sadness, self-pity, and failure capture me:

When I feel depressed, I will sing.
When I feel sad, I will laugh.
When I feel inferior, I will wear new clothes.
When I feel uncertain, I will ask questions.
When I feel poverty, I will think of the wealth to come.
When I feel incompetent, I will remember past successes.
If I feel insignificant, I will remember my goals.

Those such as depression and sadness are easy to recognize, but there are others that approach with a smile and the hand of friendship, and they too can deceive me. Against them, I must never relinquish control. Therefore, I will remember the following:

When I feel overconfident, I will recall my failures.
When I overindulge, I will think of past hungers.
When I feel complacency, I will remember my competition.
When I feel moments of greatness, I will remember moments of shame.
When I attain great wealth, I will remember those in poverty.
When I feel overly proud, I will remember a moment of weakness.

Remembering these moments will keep my life balanced. With this new knowledge I will make allowances for his or her anger and irritation of the day, for they know not the secret of controlling their thoughts. I will master my moods through positive action, and when I master my moods, I control my destiny. Today I control my destiny, and my destiny is to fulfill God's perfect will for my life.

> **Take control of your consistent emotions and begin to consciously and deliberately reshape your daily experience of life.**
>
> *Anthony Robbins*

Control Your Emotions in Every Situation

BACKGROUND:

Human emotions are a gift from God. Our emotions are pretty accurate indicators of how we are feeling on the inside. As human beings, we each go through periods where we experience different emotions at different times. The four major emotions are happiness, anger, fear, and sadness. Under those may emerge secondary emotions, such as joy, disappointment, anxiety, or depression. I feel very confident in saying that you as the reader of this sentence have experienced what each of those emotions feel like. For this activity, we shall explore the results that our own emotions and self-control (or lack of it) have had on our lives.

    A. Do you control your emotions or do you let your emotions control you?

    B. How do you handle stressful situations that cause your emotions to rise to unusual levels?

Part A:

On the lines below, recall a situation where you lost control of your emotions either internally or externally.

_____

_____

_____

_____

_____

_____

1. Do you recall what physiological changes occurred in your body while your emotions where high? If so, what were they (turning red in the face, rapid heart beat, stuttering, etc)?

_____
_____
_____

2. Did you regret losing control after everything was all over?

_____
_____
_____

3. How could you have handled the situation differently?

_____
_____
_____

4. Where do you think the habit to lose control originated? (i.e. inherited, acquired through suppression, etc.)

_____
_____
_____

5. How important do you think it is for you to maintain control of your emotions at all times? Why?

_____
_____
_____

6. What could be the negative consequences of losing control of your emotions?

_____
_____
_____

7. What could be a benefit or positive outcome of maintaining control of your emotions in difficult situations?

_____

_____

_____

8. What will you do in the future to prevent yourself from losing control of your emotions?

_____

_____

_____

Part B:

Your physical body responds to how you are feeling. For instance, if you are watching a sad movie, your body responds by falling tears and your face shows the look of sadness. If you win the lottery, your body responds by a rapid heartbeat and increased adrenalin. Your facial expression registers the emotions with widened eyes, upward lips, and a glow.

On the lines below, write what the internal and external outcome may be from experiencing the following emotions:

Example:
1. Happiness:
External – yelling with excitement, physically stronger, fresh energy, singing, dancing, smiling, humming, etc.
Internal – a feeling of gratitude and appreciation, relaxed muscles, calmness, etc.

2. Sadness:
External: _____

Internal: _____

3. Fear:
External: _____

Internal: _____

4. Anger:
External: _____

Internal: _____

5. CALMNESS is a jewel of wisdom. Its presence is an indication of wisdom. When you are calm the majority of the time, it shows that you have a very good understanding of the laws and operation of thought. When you learn how to govern yourself appropriately, you then know how to adapt yourself to everyone. They in turn respect your spiritual growth and feel that they can learn from and rely upon you.

On the lines below, write ways in which you can remain calm at most, if not all times. Make it fun!

C _____

A _____

L _____

M _____

N _____

E _____

S _____

S _____

6. As you begin practicing calmness, list the things that you can do to remain calm in intense situations.

   a. _____

   b. _____

   c. _____

   d. _____

   e. _____

7. List some places you can go to gain a sense of calmness.

   a. _____

   b. _____

   c. _____

   d. _____

   e. _____

9. On a scale of 1-10 how likely are you to do the following things in the next six months in order to relax your body and mind?

✓ Watch the sunrise?   1 2 3 4 5 6 7 8 9 10

Month that I will do this: _____

✓ Complete a good book?   1 2 3 4 5 6 7 8 9 10

Month that I will do this: _____

✓ Meditate for at least 15 minutes?   1 2 3 4 5 6 7 8 9 10

Month that I will do this: _____

✓ Relax at the pool or beach?   1 2 3 4 5 6 7 8 9 10

Month that I will do this: _____

✓ Go fishing?   1 2 3 4 5 6 7 8 9 10

Month that I will do this: _____

✓ Take a long walk?   1 2 3 4 5 6 7 8 9 10

Month that I will do this: _____

✓ Play golf?   1 2 3 4 5 6 7 8 9 10

Month that I will do this: _____

✓ Take a bubble bath?   1 2 3 4 5 6 7 8 9 10

Month that I will do this: _____

My Lessons Learned on
"Controlling Emotions"

_____
_____
_____
_____
_____
_____
_____
_____
_____
_____
_____
_____
_____
_____
_____
_____
_____
_____
_____
_____
_____
_____

Darkness cannot drive out darkness, only light can do that. Hate cannot drive out hate, only love can do that. Hate multiplies hate, violence multiplies violence, and toughness multiplies toughness in a descending spiral of destruction.

Dr. Martin Luther King, Jr.

*God is ready to give you what you have planned for,
worked for, meditated for, and prayed for.
All you have to do is reach out and grab hold of it.
You must be perceptive enough to know
when the time has arrived.*

Dr. Mia Y. Merritt

Week 6

Live Today as Your Last Day on Earth

*Why have you been allowed to live this extra day
when others far better have departed this earth?
Is it because they have accomplished their purpose in life
when yours is still yet to be achieved? Is this another
opportunity for you to become the person you
know you can be?*

*Destroy procrastination with action. Bury doubt with faith.
Dismember fear with confidence. Today is the tomorrow that
you worried about yesterday, and all is well! This moment,
this day, is as good as any moment in all eternity.
Make this day, each moment of this day,
a heaven on earth.*

*The duties of today you shall fulfill today.
Today you shall spend time with your children while they
are still here. Tomorrow they will be gone, and so will you.
Today you shall embrace your sweetheart with tender kisses;
tomorrow they will be gone, and so will you.
Today you shall lift up a friend in need;
tomorrow they will no longer need your help,
nor will you hear their request.
Today you shall give yourself in sacrifice and work;
tomorrow you will have nothing to give,
and there will be nothing to receive.*

ACTIVITY 6

> **If in my soul I know that God knows me and loves me, and loves me even though He knows me, then my heart has every reason to smile, and life is worth living.**
>
> *Author Unknown*

Live Today as Your Last Day on Earth

BACKGROUND:

Yesterday is but a dream and tomorrow is only a vision. But today well-lived, makes every yesterday a dream of happiness and every tomorrow a vision of hope. Live well therefore in this day! (author unknown). When we learn to live each day to the fullest with meaning and productivity, every day is a success. Everyone is given the same 24 hours in a day. What we do in those 24 hours sets us apart from everyone else. No two people do the same two things within a 24 hour day. Our priorities about life change when we live each day as if it were our last. Every task is performed to completion, our family and friends are given the love and affection that we have for them, and we appreciate the simple things in life that we ordinarily take for granted.

    A. What are some things that you can do now that could have a powerful impact on someone's life?

    B. If you knew that you only had one month to live, what would you do in that month?

Part A:

Begin working on the legacy that you will leave. Sow your seeds of kindness, love, peace, joy and laughter.

1. Make a list of at least five people that you can call <u>this week</u> just to tell them you love them or just to say hello (this will add sunshine to their day and they will always remember you for your thoughtfulness).

    a. _____
    b. _____
    c. _____
    d. _____
    e. _____

2. Write the names and dates of people whose birthdays you would like to remember. It makes people feel special when they get a special call on their birthday. It shows that someone is thinking of them and thinks they are worth a phone call on their special day.

January	February
_____	_____
_____	_____
_____	_____
_____	_____

March	April
_____	_____
_____	_____
_____	_____
_____	_____

May	June
_____	_____
_____	_____
_____	_____
_____	_____

July	August
_____	_____
_____	_____
_____	_____
_____	_____

September	October
_____	_____
_____	_____
_____	_____
_____	_____

November	December
_____	_____
_____	_____
_____	_____
_____	_____

> *You may think that remembering someone's birthday is a small token of love, but you have no idea how much of an impact that phone call can have on someone's life. People remember the little things. Sow seeds of love and kindness. They will come back to you multiplied. Sow your seeds everyday in various ways. Make sure that you will be pleased with the harvest when it sprouts.*

Part B:

If you knew that you only had one month to live, what would you do in that month?

1. On the lines below, write all the things that you would do if you knew that you only had one month to live.

_____
_____
_____
_____
_____
_____
_____
_____

> *All human beings go through periods of birth, growth, fruitage, and decline. One day we all shall die. We shall return back to the dust from whence we came. However, we want to leave not only a memory in the hearts and minds of our family and friends, but a legacy to the world. What do you want your legacy to be? Preparing for the end does not make it imminent. Be optimistic, but also realistic.*

In the exercises below, make a list of all the things you want to <u>have</u>, <u>do</u>, or <u>be</u> before you depart from this earth.

2. I would like to have possessed the following before I make my transition from earth (i.e. wisdom, courage, joy, a big home, a luxurious car, a yacht, etc.) It does not necessarily have to be materialistic:

_____

_____

_____

_____

3. I would like to have done the following (i.e. traveled the world, written a book, opened a school, etc.):

_____

_____

_____

_____

4. I would like to have exhibited the following predominant characteristics (i.e. bold, kind, compassionate, generous, etc.):

_____

_____

_____

_____

5. What legacy would you like to leave for the world to let them know that you were here (a foundation, a book, something named after me, my children, etc):

_____

_____

_____

_____

6. Make a list of all the people that you would call to <u>ask for forgiveness</u> for a wrong or past hurt that you caused them.

    a. _____

    b. _____

    c. _____

    d. _____

7. Make a list of the people that you would call to <u>forgive</u> for some wrong or hurt that they caused you (they may not even know that they hurt you).

    a. _____

    b. _____

    c. _____

    d. _____

8. If you would leave a letter for someone to read after you died, who would that letter be written to? _____. On the next page, write what you would say in that letter:

> Humm, what should I say?
> Well, I need to do the following:
>
> ➢ Be honest and sincere
> ➢ Be heartfelt
> ➢ Leave a lasting impression
> ➢ End on a positive note

Letter to: _____

From: _____ **Date:** _____

My Lessons Learned on
"Living Today as Your Last Day on Earth"

Some people drift through their entire life. They do it one day at a time, one week at a time, one month at a time. It happens so gradually that they are unaware of how their lives are slipping away until it's too late.

Mary Kay Ash

Week 7

Believe That You Are a Miracle

God danced the day you were born! Since the beginning of time there has never been another with your mind, your heart, your eyes, your ears, your hands, your hair, your mouth. No one who came before, no one who lives today, and no one who comes tomorrow will walk and talk and move exactly like you! You are rare, and there is value in rarity, therefore you are valuable!

Don't look for miracles because you are a miracle. Don't compare yourself with others because you are a unique and beautiful creation. Don't let yesterday's accomplishments be sufficient for today's commitments, nor should you indulge anymore in self-praise for deeds, which in reality are too small to even acknowledge.

You are here for a purpose and that purpose is to grow into a mountain, not to shrink to a grain of sand. Henceforth, you will apply all your efforts to become the highest mountain of all, and you will strain your potential until it cries for mercy!

Seek constantly to improve your manners and graces, for they are the sugar to which all are attracted.

Your problems, discouragements and heartaches are really great opportunities in disguise. You should no longer be fooled by the natural garments they wear because your eyes are open wide. Look beyond the natural and do not be deceived.

ACTIVITY #7

> **God Made You an Original Not a Copy.
> Be Yourself.**
>
> *Author Unknown*

Believe That You Are a Miracle

BACKGROUND:
Humanity is made up of innumerable individuals, but no two are alike. We are to unify ourselves with each other in love and peace while expressing our individualities, but being unified with mankind does not mean uniformity. Every flower, every tree, every blade of grass, every drop of water, every snowflake is a little different than any other one of its counterparts. You are rare, and there is value in rarity, therefore you are valuable! Don't look for miracles because *you* are a miracle. Do not compare yourself with others because you are a unique and beautiful creation.

    A. If you were asked to describe yourself in three adjectives, what would you say? How do you really see yourself?

    B. Examine yourself and think about the different roles you play in the lives of others. How would you define those roles?

Part A:

1. On the lines below, describe yourself in three adjectives. Don't think too hard about it. Just write the first three words that come to your mind. Those are usually the most honest.

    a. _____

    b. _____

    c. _____

2. If someone were to ask you to tell them a little about yourself, what would you say? Write how you would describe yourself on the lines that follow:

_____
_____
_____
_____
_____
_____
_____
_____

> *In writing your three adjectives and describing yourself, did you depict yourself in terms of your appearance, your abilities, your outlook on life, or a combination of those things? Most people would assess themselves in terms of the roles they play in the lives of others, (i.e. a parent, a spouse, an employee, a boss, a daughter or a friend). Some of your word choices probably included your relationships with others (i.e. loyal, faithful, caring, etc.) This simple exercise helps you to define the person you "think" you are.*

3. Name three unique characteristics about yourself that set you apart from others?

   a. _____

   b. _____

   c. _____

4. Write down three of your strengths.

   a. _____

   b. _____

   c. _____

5. Why do you feel that these are strengths?

_____
_____
_____

6. On the lines below, write down three of your weaknesses.

   a. _____

   b. _____

   c. _____

7. Why do you feel that these are weaknesses?

   _____

   _____

   _____

8. What are your greatest fears?

   a. _____

   b. _____

   c. _____

9. From where or how do you think these fears came?

   a. _____

   b. _____

   c. _____

10. How do you think you can overcome your fears?

    _____

    _____

    _____

11. How will you overcome them?

    _____

    _____

    _____

I once saw an acronym for the word fear:

F E A R: **F**alse **E**xpectations **A**ppearing **R**eal.

Once you overcome your "false expectations" and go after your goals with running shoes on, you will begin to do things you never imagined were possible. Fearlessness removes all fear.

One of the most profound quotes on fear that I have ever read comes from ***Marianne Williamson*** in the following. You probably have heard it before:

> ***OUR DEEPEST FEAR***
> *Our deepest fear is not that we are inadequate. Our deepest fear is that we are powerful beyond measure. It is our light, not our darkness that most frightens us. We ask ourselves, Who am I to be brilliant, gorgeous, talented, and fabulous? Actually, who are you not to be? You are a child of God. Your playing small does not serve the world. There is nothing enlightened about shrinking so that other people won't feel insecure around you. We are all meant to shine, as children do. We were born to make manifest the glory of God that is within us. It's not just in some of us; it's in everyone. And as we let our own light shine, we unconsciously give other people permission to do the same. As we are liberated from our own fear, our presence automatically liberates others.*

Part B:

Dave Weber, author of the book *Sticks and Stones* defined seven concepts of self. He states that each of these concepts lives inside of us and help define the person we are. According to him, our composite as human beings results from the integration of the seven concepts. Those concepts are the following:

The Seven Me's

- The Me I Think I am
- The Me I Really am
- The Me I Use to Be
- The Me That Others see
- The Me I Try to Project
- The Me Others Try to Make Me
- The Me I Want to Be

> *You probably never really looked at your life this way, but if you are honest with yourself, you can agree that there are at least five of these "Me's" in you. On the lines below, try and describe each one.*

1. The "Me" I Think I am.

___

2. The "Me" I really am.

___

3. The "Me" I Use to be.

___

4. The "Me" that others see.

___

5. The "Me I try to project.

_____
_____
_____
_____
_____

6. The "Me" that others try to make me.

_____
_____
_____
_____
_____

7. The "Me I want to be (This should correspond with the affirmation that you wrote on page 24).

_____
_____
_____
_____
_____
_____
_____
_____
_____

My Lessons Learned on
"Believing That You Are a Miracle"

There is something special within you, a basic goodness that you must choose to manifest in every way you can.

Les Brown

*Your goals are a stimulating pursuit.
When you develop goals, you are actually planning
how you want your life to be in terms of what
you want to see manifested.*

Dr. Mia Y. Merritt

Week 8

Plan for Prosperity and Abundance

*With persistence comes success. You must
persist no matter how slow you have to move at first.
No one enjoys great achievement without passing the persistence test.
Those who can endure are greatly rewarded for their
persistence. They receive as their reward,
whatever goal they are pursuing.*

*Lack of persistence is one of the greatest causes
of failure. You must work. You must endure.
You must ignore the obstacles at your feet and keep
your eyes on the goals in front of you. You may still
encounter failure, yet success hides behind the next corner.
Strain your potential until it cries for mercy.*

*Dream big dreams! Reach for the moon,
and even if you miss, you will land among the stars!
It is better to attempt to do something great and fail,
than attempt to do nothing and succeed.*

*Before success comes in your life, you will meet
with temporary defeat and even some failure,
but success will come just one step beyond that point
at which momentary defeat tries to overtake you.
Temporary defeat is NOT permanent failure!
A very large portion of your success will come from
eating the bread of adversity, and drinking the
waters of affliction.*

> What we see with the natural eye already exists in the physical world, but what we see when we visualize, already exists in the spiritual world. We must bring what we see in the spiritual world out of the invisible into the visible.
> *Charles Haanal*

Plan for Prosperity and Abundance

BACKGROUND:
People are looking at you and wondering if you truly believe in your vision, your goals, and your dreams. If you are not positive, if you are not confident, if you are not excited about your own aspirations, how can you expect anyone else to be excited for you? When you work with diligence towards your goals, people notice, and they support you and your vision. Everything you do will make an impression on others. Therefore, it is of the utmost importance that you begin to value yourself as an individual worthy of accomplishing great things.

   A. Have you identified meaningful goals in life that you would like to see accomplished?

   B. Do you watch that the words which proceed from your mouth are positive and encouraging?

Part A:
On the lines below, identify at least three major goals in each area that you would like to accomplish within the next six months. Make sure that your goals are challenging and realistic.

Under each goal, there are spaces provided for you to write action plans to describe how you will accomplish these goals. For instance, if your goal was to take two classes at the local university, then your goal and action plan should look something like this:

EDUCATIONAL GOAL:
   1. Complete two classes at the local university in six months.

   Action Plan:
   a. Register for classes during the Fall registration
   b. Purchase books needed for both classes.

Setting goals gives meaning to your life. With goals to work towards, you are always striving to grow, develop, and get better. On the lines below, set at least three goals in each of the areas below:

SPIRITUAL

1. _____
2. _____
3. _____

Action Plan:

a. _____
b. _____
c. _____

FINANCIAL

1. _____
2. _____
3. _____

Action plan:

a. _____
b. _____
c. _____

EDUCATIONAL

1. _____
2. _____
3. _____

Action Plan:

a. _____
b. _____
c. _____

HEALTH

1. _____
2. _____
3. _____

Action plan:

a. _____
b. _____
c. _____

PERSONAL

1. _____
2. _____
3. _____

Action Plan:

a. _____
b. _____
c. _____

RECREATIONAL

1. _____
2. _____
3. _____

Action plan:

a. _____
b. _____
c. _____

FAMILY   **CAREER**

1. _____   1. _____
2. _____   2. _____
3. _____   3. _____

<u>Action Plan:</u>   <u>Action plan:</u>

a. _____   a. _____
b. _____   b. _____
c. _____   c. _____

> *When you have a clear vision of the person you intend to become and you have distinct goals written to help you become that person, your life has meaning. Small, insignificant things no longer bother you because your eyes are on the goals in front of you.*

You may use this same format for writing one year goals, monthly, goals or weekly goals. They may look something like this:

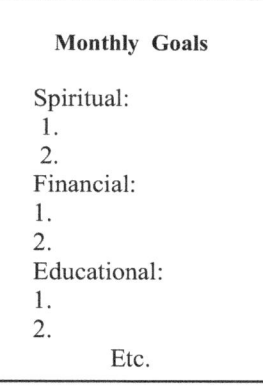

Writing goals can help you to identify other areas in your life where there are gifts, talents, and abilities. Your gifts can also be used to bring additional income to you. Money circles help you identify different ways in which you may bring income into your life through your God-given talents. In the center of the circle, write your primary source of income. In the outer circles, write other ways in which you can make money. Then, you must make the time to pursue those other areas in order to bring additional cash flow into your life.

Take a look at the money circles on the next page. Use them to see how you can identify areas that will benefit you in a monetary way.

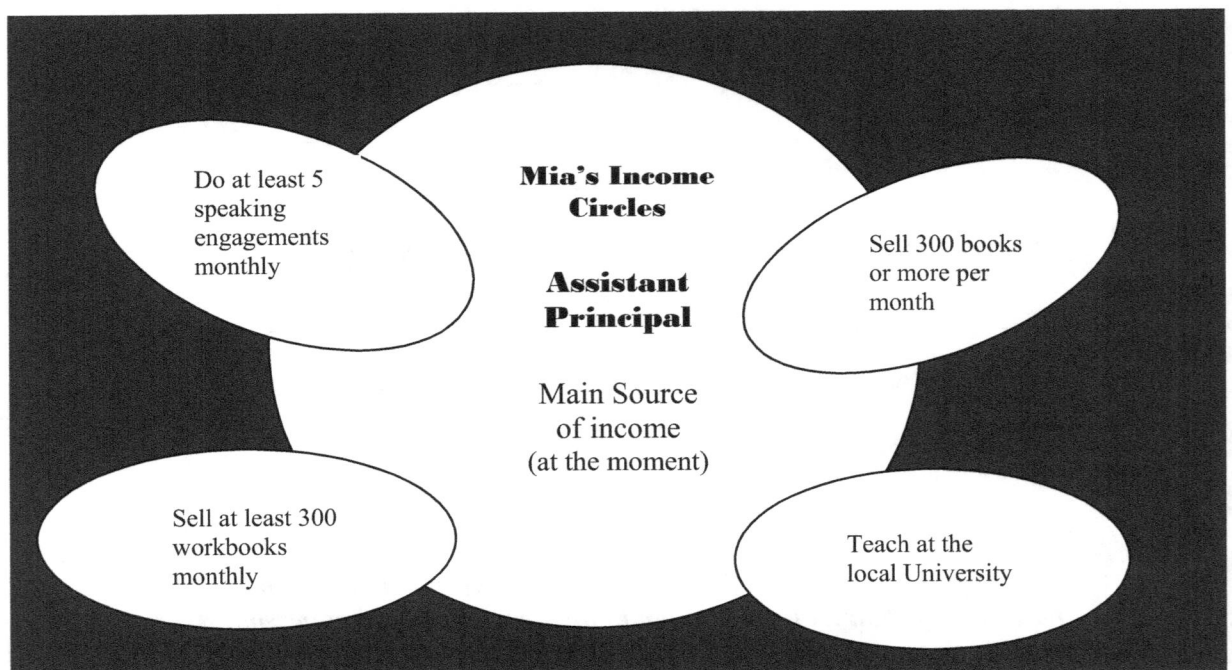

Fill in your money circles below:

Part B:

Do you guard the words that you speak? Are they positive and encouraging? Everything in your world revolves around your words and thoughts. The words you speak are constantly creating your future. Your word speaks and your word becomes law and law becomes cause and effect. There is life-giving power spoken in every word. There is something that always comes back to you through the words you speak. Words are the first manifestation of thought. This wonderful power of clothing thoughts in the form of words is what separates humans from the animal kingdom. Words can heal our hurts or breathe life into seemingly dead situations. Words literally create realities for us.

Study the definitions for the following eight words below.

1. **Affirm** – To insist or maintain to be true
2. **Claim** – A demand for what is rightfully due
3. **Command** – To be in control of or authority over
4. **Declare** – To say forcefully and make known to be
5. **Decree** - A formal order or decision
6. **Mandate** – An authoritive command
7. **Proclaim** – To announce publicly, make known, declare
8. **Pronounce** – To declare officially or solemnly

Now use each word in a sentence. Make sure that your sentence reveals the truth of what you want to see manifested in your life. After you have written your sentences, repeat each one over and over until if fills your consciousness. Try and do this at least once per day.

Example:

I affirm the presence of prosperity all around me. I receive it and I identify myself with it.

1. **Affirm:**
_____
_____
_____

2. **Claim:**
_____
_____
_____

3. **Command:**

4. **Declare:**

5. **Decree:**

6. **Mandate:**

7. **Proclaim:**

8. **Pronounce:**

My Lessons Learned on
"Planning for Prosperity & Abundance"

The secret to productive goal setting is establishing clearly defined goals, writing them down and then focusing on them several times a day with words and emotions as if we've already achieved them.

Denis Waitley

*At the end of each day before you prepare to rest,
an inventory of the day's events should be done and
the review of the day should be pleasant and productive.*

Dr. Mia Y. Merritt

Week 9

Examine Each Night Your Deeds of the Day

At each day's end, I will carefully examine the progress and problems of my day's journey, and this will create in my mind a diary for today, and textbook for tomorrow.

In the evening before I retire, I will review the words and actions of every hour of the day, and I will allow nothing to escape my examination, for why should I fear the sight of my errors when I have the power to admonish and forgive myself?

Perhaps I was too cutting in a certain dispute. My opinion could have been withheld, for it stung but did no good. What I said may have been true, but all truths are not to be spoken at all times. I should have held my tongue, for there is no contending either with fools or superiors.

Am I guilty of omission? Was there something I could have done to help someone or a situation, but I neglected to do so? Am I guilty of commission? Did I deliberately do or say something that was not appropriate, nor fruit bearing?

Let me review my actions. Let me observe myself as my greatest enemy might do, and I will become my own best friend. I will begin right now, to become what I will be hereafter. Darkness may fall, but sleep will not cover my eyes until I have reviewed in full the events of my day.

> **A moral being is one who is capable of reflecting on his past actions and their motives – of approving of some and disapproving of others.**
>
> *Charles Darwin*

Reflect on Your Deeds of Each Day

BACKGROUND:
Reflection is a process of self-examination and self-evaluation of a person's actions, behaviors, responses, and interactions. John Dewey asserted that reflection is an important aspect of learning from experiences. When one takes the time to reflect on the words and actions of the day and honestly points out any errors while striving to correct them in the days to come, one is well on his or her way to becoming a great person to a very significant degree.

A. There are some commendable things that you do on a daily basis. This could be at work, at home, at worship service or wherever you go. These things help contribute to you being a more successful and fulfilled person.

B. As you look back over your life, you will realize that you have done so many things and met many people. This information tells you a lot about yourself and the person that you are.

Part A:

Make a list of the things that you do daily, such as pray, problem solving, returning phone calls, responding to e-mails, etc. You may not even realize that what you do really makes a difference. Think about a typical day and make a list of the habits that you practice which helps you to recognize who you are as a person.

1. _____

2. _____

3. _____

4. _____

Look back at the list that you wrote and write a brief statement of how each of these habits help you to be productive. Your answers on the following lines should correspond to the actions that you wrote in the preceding lines.

1._____

2._____

3._____

4._____

Part B:

The things you know, things that you can do, people you know, things you have owned, currently own, and the positions that you have held in the past all contribute to the way you see things now. As you take all your combined experiences, they help you to understand why you do things the way you do today. They also help you when reflecting on your actions and thoughts from each day's events.

On the lines below, take an inventory of yourself in order to recognize your potential.

THINGS I KNOW:
You are to list the things you have knowledge of. This is what the average person does not know (i.e. the health field, sewing, animals, real estate, poetry, opening a business, etc.).

1._____

2._____

3._____

4._____

THINGS I CAN DO:
Here you are to list things that you can do that the average person can not, (i.e. belly dance, build a house, fly a plane, change a car engine, rap, juggle, etc.)

1._____

2._____

3._____

4._____

THINGS I OWN:
Here you are to list things that you own that the average person does not *(i.e. a pet snake, a 1956 Chevy, a Mona Lisa painting, a theater in your home, etc.)*

1. _____

2. _____

3. _____

4. _____

PEOPLE I KNOW:
Here you are to list the names of people you know or have met that the average person has not *(i.e. Oprah Winfrey, Tom Hanks, the president of your organization, a famous athlete, politician, a famous person, etc.)*

1. _____

2. _____

3. _____

4. _____

JOBS I HAVE HAD:
Here you are to list the jobs you have had that the average person has not *(a bouncer in a club, an FBI agent, a clown at the circus, a public official, etc)*

1. _____

2. _____

3. _____

4. _____

THINGS THAT PEOPLE TELL ME:
Here you are to list things that people tell you that they don't tell the average person (i.e. marital problems, health issues, children concerns, situations with friends, etc.)

1. _____

2. _____

3. _____

4. _____

THINGS I HAVE DONE:
Here you are to list things that you have done that the average person probably has not done. (i.e. traveled the world, performed on Broadway, appeared in a TV commercial, jumped out of an airplane, etc.)

1. _____

2. _____

3. _____

4. _____

THINGS THAT ARE GREAT ABOUT ME:
Here you are to list the great things about you that most people don't know.

1. _____

2. _____

3. _____

4. _____

THINGS I AM SENSTIVE ABOUT:
Here you are to list the great things that make you emotional, bring tears to your eyes, or cause you to become vulnerable or afraid.

1. _____

2. _____

3. _____

4. _____

> This exercise should have given you a lot to remember. As you look back over the list, you should be amazed at the things that are on it. This information tells you things about yourself and contributes to the person that you are. You have experienced a lot and oftentimes you don't reflect on all the things you own, heard, or seen. If the list is not impressive, then as long as you wake up each and everyday with your health you can change what is to transpire in that day. You are the master of your destiny. You are the captain of your ship.

My Lessons Learned on
"Reflecting on Your Deeds of Each Day"

Most true happiness comes from one's inner life, from the disposition of the mind and soul. Admittedly, a good inner life is difficult to achieve, especially in these trying times. It takes reflection and contemplation and self-discipline.

William L Shirer

Week 10

Pray With an Attitude of Gratitude

I will pray for guidance.

*Heavenly Father,
I come to you in humble submission to honor, worship,
praise, and magnify your holy and righteous name. I thank you for life,
health, strength, and the wisdom to know that you are to be magnified and
honored in my life. I thank you for putting the spiritual strength and fortitude
inside me, which has enabled me to overcome every trial, tribulation,
hardship and difficulty in my life. Each encounter has made me stronger,
better, and wiser. Each victory has increased my faith in you to deliver me
out of every seeming impossibility.*

*Lord, please continue to teach me how to live this life with faith, courage,
integrity, grace, and confidence. Allow me a forgiving heart and mind that
will lead me on the path that keeps me free and strong. Help me to always
strive for the highest legitimate reward of merit, ambition, and opportunity;
but never allow me to forget to extend a kind, helping hand to others who
need encouragement and assistance.*

*Lord, I ask for wisdom to acknowledge rewards and recognition with humility.
Let the spirit of excellence, understanding and patience take
root in my heart, mind and soul manifesting through actions, words,
and deeds. Keep me forever serene in every activity of life. Allow me to
possess a tranquil heart that will keep me calm regardless of unfavorable
circumstances. In sorrow, may my soul be uplifted by the thought
that if there were no shadow, there would be no sunshine. Steady me to
do the full share of my work and more with efficiency and effectiveness,
and when that is done, stop me. Pay what wages thou will, and permit
me to say from a loving heart, a grateful
………AMEN.*

> Sincere gratitude empowers you to focus on the positive aspects of life, and develops into greater awareness and appreciation of the overlooked, often misinterpreted, and ever so important little blessings that make up this experience we call life.
>
> *unknown*

Gratitude

BACKGROUND:
Gratitude is opening your heart to be thankful for life and all the past and present things that you have experienced. It is realizing that as you continue to live, there is a reason to be thankful. Gratitude is an emotional vibration that goes out into the universe and causes your desires to quickly manifest. Feeling in a positive way about the "now" and being thankful about the present puts you in sync with things that you desire. The more grateful you fix your mind upon God and all that He has done for you, the more good things you will receive and the faster they will come. The mental attitude of gratitude draws your mind in closer touch with God than the one who never looks to him with a thankful heart.

A. Have you pondered over all the things that you are grateful for? Have you given thanks to God for the good and bad from the past and present having faith in His ability to guide you in the future?

B. If you were to read your obituary before you died, would you be pleased with what it would say? What would you like to be written in your obituary after you died?

Part A:
Make a list of the things that you are grateful for. Start with right now and go back as far as you can. Be sure to "feel" the gratitude for those things that you write down. If you don't feel gratitude for it, do not write it. You must be truly thankful.

MY GRATITUDE LIST

1. _____
2. _____
3. _____
4. _____
5. _____
6. _____
7. _____
8. _____
9. _____
10. _____
11. _____
12. _____
13. _____
14. _____
15. _____
16. _____
17. _____
18. _____
19. _____
20. _____

Part B:
Some people have been told that they were soon to depart from this earth. After accepting and processing this revelation, it actually gives them some time to prepare and get some things in order including their final arrangements. If you had a chance to write your obituary, what would you want it to say? On the lines below, write what you would want people to read from your obituary.

OBITUARY FOR

_____

_____

_____

_____

_____

_____

_____

_____

_____

_____

_____

_____

_____

_____

_____

_____

_____

My Lessons Learned on "Gratitude"

Develop an attitude of gratitude, and give thanks for everything that happens to you, knowing that every step forward is a step toward achieving something bigger and better than your current situation.

Brian Tracy

Destined for Great Things Workbook
Author: Dr. Mia Y. Merritt
www.Miamerritt.com

M&M Inspirational Consulting
www.destinedforgreatthings.com
Dr. Mia Y. Merritt
President/CEO
1-866-560-7652

Books written by Mia Merritt:
Destined for Great Things!
Prosperity is my Birthright!

For information on Mastermind,
please contact
www.internationalmasterminders.com
for membership information
President: Ann McNeil